The Great ReEvaluation
Integration Guide

MARK E. TIDSWORTH

Copyright © 2023 Pinnacle Leadership Press

All rights reserved. No part of this publication may be reproduced, stored in a retrieval system or transmitted in any way by any means, electronic, mechanical, photocopy, recording or otherwise, without the prior permission of the author, except as provided by USA copyright law.

www.pinnlead.com/pl-press

ISBN:

CONTENTS

Using This Integration Guide	3
Two Foundational Truths	5
The Great ReEvaluation is Underway	7
What This Means for Churches	11
Leading Transformation Entering the Adaptive Zone	15
Clarifying the Why and What	21
Switching to Discovery Mode	27
Boldly Proceeding with Confidence	33
Adapting As They Go	37
Thriving Churches	41

The Great ReEvaluation Integration Guide
A Church Leadership Growth Experience For
Clergy, Church Staff, and Lay Leaders

Welcome to The Great ReEvaluation Course!
Your willingness to participate, giving of your time and energy to this growth experience, is a gift to us all in this Christian movement. We hope you will personally be enriched, and your church will become a greater expression of the body of Christ as a result. Thank you.

Using This Integration Guide

Assurance and freedom. These are our aspirations for this Integrations Guide. By providing this guide, with the basic content of this Course included, we hope this gives you the assurance you have access to this content already. Thus, there is no need for excessive note taking or content capturing during our sessions together. Instead, this guide gives you freedom to engage the action of the sessions with assurance you aren't missing content. We are hopeful this assurance and freedom will equip you to maximize the benefit of this growth experience.

As we were developing this guide, our first inclination was to use the title *The Great ReEvaluation Workbook*, which would be straightforward and descriptive. With reflection though, we chose the current title, using the word *Integration* with purpose. Our hope is that this guide will lead you toward personal growth as a disciple of Jesus Christ while providing opportunity for your church to also engage transformation. We could have named this *The Action Guide* and remained true to our intent.

This integration focus explains the numerous Discovery Points and Pivot Points interspersed throughout. We may touch on them during our sessions, yet they are primarily designed for you and your church leadership team to engage afterwards. As we go, you may want to write thoughts, ideas, or reactions in the margins, but these Discovery and Pivot Points require more engagement than we can do during our gatherings. At the end of each session, there is space available for you to harvest the Discoveries and Pivots to discuss with your leadership team, facilitating missional movement.

Discovery Points
These are opportunities to stop, reflect, pray, listen, discuss, and record your insights.

Pivot Points
These are opportunities to consider pivots you personally or your church may make toward centering in the Way of Jesus.

Two Foundational Truths

1 - The Way of Jesus is winsome and beautiful

- A hopeful vision for planet earth
- A sustainable, enduring way of being & living while in volatile times
- A proactive way to order our days, a guiding life-ethic
- A pathway and power for personal and corporate transformation

Discovery Point

What might the author mean by "the Way of Jesus," and from where does this description of the Jesus-Way of life come?

Winsome and beautiful...two words describing a positive, life-giving, attractive way of being in the world. How in touch with the winsomeness and beauty of your faith are you at this point in your spiritual journey?

How about your church? How much does it seem your church animated by a winsome and beautiful version of the Way of Jesus?
When your answer is affirmative, celebrate and carry on, enjoying the ride.

When your answer raises concerns, this may be a good time to talk with someone you trust about how you personally might reconnect with the pearl of great price or treasure buried in the field, so to speak. Or when your church is less in touch with the Way of Jesus than you would hope, raising this awareness with each other is a starting point toward vitalization.

2 - There is a Savior for God's Church, and it's not us

> ¹ God is our refuge and strength,
>   a very present[a] help in trouble.
> ² Therefore we will not fear, though the earth should change,
>   though the mountains shake in the heart of the sea,
> ³ though its waters roar and foam,
>   though the mountains tremble with its tumult. *Selah*
> ⁴ There is a river whose streams make glad the city of God,
>   the holy habitation of the Most High.
>   Psalm 46, NRSV

 Discovery Point

Relief...thanks be to God we don't have to create the energy for being nor doing church. God provides the power, while our role is to trust ourselves to God's strength. How would you, your leadership team, and church be different were you more trusting, drawing your strength from the Holy Spirit rather than trying to "make things happen" yourselves?

The Great ReEvaluation Is Underway

You are not alone. If you are rethinking your approach to life these days, you are not alone. The extreme volatility in the world as we know it is pushing us way out of our comfort zones. Assumption disruption is in full swing. Our values, commitments, alliances, and beliefs are shaken and sifted as we endure ongoing chronic stress from large-scale disruption events.

Signals From The World of Work
"From organizational research, we know that when human beings come into contact with death and illness in their lives, it causes them to take a step back and ask existential questions. Like, what gives me purpose and happiness in life, and does that match up with how I'm spending my right now? So, in many cases, those reflections will lead to life pivots." -Insider Online Magazine, Juliana Kaplan, October 2, 2021

During times of great volatility, existential questions arise, leading to reevaluation of most everything

>Marriage and significant other relationships
>Parent – child relationships
>Friendships
>Vocations and workplaces
>Where we live
>How we live
>And even faith and church life

Everything around us is changing and the Great ReEvaluation is underway

Discovery Point

Personally, how has the Great ReEvaluation been real for you? Looking back, what pivots have you made? How are you different as a person now as a result of the recent volatility in our world?

How is your church different now? What pivots or changes have been made in the last three years?

The Current Situation – Church Trends

- *Exploring the Pandemic's Effect on Congregations, A Webinar, April 2022. Presented by Researchers from Hartford International University, Lilly Funded*
- *Twenty Years of Congregational Change: The 2020 Faith Communities Today Overview, Hartford Institute for Religion Research, Hartford International Seminary*

Tracking trends since 2000
This survey included 15,278 religious communities, 80 denominations
This particular survey tracked religious communities from 2015-2020

2015-2020 Survey Results
- Size churches (measured by worship attendance)
  Median size 20 years ago = 137
  Median size now = 65
- Means that half of all churches have 65 or less who attend worship
- 70% of attenders are in the largest 10% of churches

Post-Pandemic Survey Results, April 2022
- "20-50% of congregations are growing"
- Now, 52% are below pre-pandemic attendance levels
- Smaller churches are the most threatened by the pandemic's effects
- Worship - 80% are now in hybrid worship with 15% with only in-person worship
- Volunteering - Pre-pandemic, congregations reported that 44% of their people volunteered in or through their church. Post-pandemic, congregations reported that 20% of their people volunteered in or through their church
- Financial Contributions - 41% of congregations saw their giving increase during the pandemic, with most returning to pre-pandemic levels now

Discovery Point

This information is based on larger surveys of many churches. Your church is not fully described by these descriptions. Yet, these serve as trend lines for many churches. What insights do these trend lines raise regarding your church? What's insights are here for you to see? Currently, you don't have to know what to do about your insights, yet this is an opportune moment for capturing your insights.

What This Means For Churches

This is a unique, critical, and opportune time for God's Church
- Our world has been making the shift from the Modern to Post-Modern Era since the year 2000 or so – large-scale, massive overhaul in every area of life. See *The Great Emergence* by Phyllis Tickle and *Shift* by Mark Tidsworth
- We have never come out of a major pandemic before, during our lifetimes.
- Overall, the way we were being and doing church before the Pandemic was not working so well; a paradigm in decline

Six Expectations For Post-Pandemic Church AND Beyond

Expect relationship shifting, given the deep hunger for authentic and genuine community

Expect a ravenous hunger for robust spiritual enrichment

Expect participation pattern shifting

Expect resignations from and volunteering for church leadership

Expect structural breakdown and organizational re-formation

Expect more truth-telling and less truth-avoiding

Pivot Point

How about you personally? Which of these six expectation descriptions describes pivots you have made or your spiritual condition (like ravenous hunger for spiritual enrichment)? After you answer, what might this mean for you? What pivots might you make?

How do you see these expectations playing out in your church to date?

What Churches Must Refuse To Do
- Live off lingering nostalgic memories of previous success
- Try recreating a bygone era which appreciates church-as-we-knew-it
- Expect Christendom culture to feed us members, while we passively stand by
- Tolerate mission-drift, energy draining institutionalism, or bloated organizational structures
- Continue irrelevant church practices, ministries, or programs
- Fearfully ignore the current concerns in the marketplace

What Churches Must Pursue
- Connect the deep spiritual hunger in our world with the robust Way of Jesus
- Live and contribute a winsome, different, and hopeful way of being in this world
- Accept that returning to church-as-we-have-known-it is impossible, accepting there is no going back anymore
- Proactively pursue this unprecedented transformation opportunity, entering the adaptive zone, making the most of this current opportunity
- Refining and affirming their mission, pursuing essential church
- Engage and welcome people wherever they are in their faith journey

Discovery Point

Capture any insights rising from the content above here, preserving for exploration and consideration with your leadership team.

We at Pinnacle Leadership Associates are observing outcomes of the Great ReEvaluation in churches. People are sorting themselves into four distinct groupings, approaching their relationships with their churches from one of four perspectives or approaches. These are not exclusive nor exhaustive approaches; I'm sure there are others or nuances of these. Yet these four are making regular appearances in (or out of) the churches with whom we are engaging.

The Accepters
- Experience church as unsatisfying
- Discouraged about their church's future, low hope
- Remain part of the church regardless due to various motivations
- Accepting what is, with low-level ongoing disappointment

The Affirmers
- Appreciate their church and how it functions
- Healthy Affirmers can look critically at their church, while unhealthy Affirmers perceive criticism as disloyalty
- Mostly uncritical, appreciative participation

The Reshapers
- Volatility has served to invigorate their faith and inspire new visions for being church
- Determined to discover the next expression of church as it unfolds
- Unwilling to accept status quo church-as-we-have-known-it
- Focused on the reshaping of church into greater expressions of body of Christ

The Leavers
- Volatility drained their motivations for church participation, creating Dones
- Volatility revved their faith, making them discontent with church-as-we-have-known-it (like Reshapers)
- Believe their church will not adapt, change, or transform
- They have left or are still barely engaged

I hope this is a realistic and accurate view of how people are sorting themselves in relation to their churches. Of course we could identify additional approaches. Of course most of us are a mix of approaches, identifying with more than one. My hope is that raising our awareness about these four approaches will help us assess the vitality and trajectory of our churches, positioning us to become greater expressions of the body of Christ.

Discovery Point

So, why did you return? What is it about being part of your church that you made the choice to return to (or continue) engagement at some level? Far too many decided not to re-engage, yet you did. What's that about? Consider sharing your answers with your leadership team, helping them to know you better while being encouraged about your church's journey.

Since the Great ReEvaluation is underway, and since that includes reevaluating relationships with church, how does this awareness inform and guide your leadership?

The Great ReEvaluation is underway
And this is perfect timing for God's Church
The greatest church transformation and vitalization opportunity of our lifetime is right before us.

Compelling church required!

Leading Transformation
Entering The Adaptive Zone

Our Aspiration
Cultivating Churches to Become Communities of Transformation

Three Prerequisites for Leading Church Transformation
Pinnacle is all about Adaptive Transformation and our experience tells us 3 prerequisites are necessary in order to lead mission-congruent transformation

1. Love – Does, can, and will our church leadership love us?
2. Competence – Is our church leadership competent in basic Churchcraft
3. Trust – Do we trust our church leadership enough to step out of our comfort zones into mission-congruent risk?

Discovery Point
Look over all three of these prerequisites. Using a 0-10 scale (0 low and 10 high) rate the level of each in your church from your perspective. Of course, this is awkward and doesn't allow for nuance. When you discuss your numbers with your leadership team, you can describe your perspective more fully.

Love –

Competence –

Trust –

Describing Success

What do churches need from leadership in order to move forward toward thriving during The Great ReEvaluation?

Motivated leaders are interested in what success or effectiveness means and looks like
Success is when churches become transformational communities......forming individuals, churches, and communities in the Way of Jesus

 Discovery Point

What do you think about the author's definition of success? Does it include the Great Commission (Matthew 28) and the New Commandment (John 13)? How do you personally define church success?

How does your church define success? How well does your answer align with your church's stated mission? What does this suggest to you as the leadership team?

To serve as effective Faith Change Agents
Transformational leaders will need to update self-perceptions, embracing a different primary paradigm for church leadership

Faith Change Agent – A New Church Leadership Paradigm
- Faith = Current in which we swim, Story we are living, "Alive in the Adventure of Jesus"
- Change Agent = Primary role is to initiate, cultivate, facilitate, and otherwise lead this group to transform; moving from this to that
- Faith Community Change Agent = Leading the church transformation process toward a more robust, faithful, and relevant expression of itself
- Primary Calling – To help this church move from here to there; from church-as-we-have-known-it to church-as-it-is-becoming

Biblical Faith Change Agents
- Moses: Transition from Egypt to Promised Land, from enslaved people to a free people
- Joshua: Transition from nomadic people to conquering people
- Peter, James: Transition from establishment religion to spiritual movement
- Paul: Transition from Jews only salvation to salvation for all (Gentiles included)

Describing Faith Change Agents

- Driven by love; love for God, God's Church, and humankind
- Carry an accurate understanding of what's happening in the current situation
- Committed to maximizing this critical transformation opportunity
- Perceive their callings as shepherding churches through this transition to become transformational churches
- Eager to cultivate transformational church community and culture

 Pivot Point

How are you responding to the Faith Change Agent church leadership paradigm? How much to do you see yourself this way? Is this what the church needs from its leadership during the Great ReEvaluation? What would this mean for you were you to embrace this paradigm for your leadership?

Suppose your leadership team embraces the role of Faith Change Agents…
How would this influence what you do? How would you communicate this with your church? How would this shift or change your team meetings?

Getting Ourselves To Good Space

Living in the Way of Jesus is beautiful, a life-giving, winsome, and invigorating way to be in this world.

Leaders are simultaneously
- exhausted and invigorated
- overwhelmed and liberated
- resistant and ready

 Discovery Point

It's been a crazy ride in recent years for us all here on planet earth. The pandemic was over, and then it wasn't, was over again, and then it wasn't. The new normal when it comes to our climate is change, with former weather patterns shifting. So how are you in this current situation? Looking at the three bullet points above, with which do you resonate? Are you more caught in the past, held back by real yet problematic feelings and experiences? Are you more engaged in the present, eager to make the most of the transformation opportunities before us? Both?

Three Timely Truths For Church Leadership

> 1 - Leadership is real - and required for churches to function, pursuing their callings and joining God's transformational mission. Churches will find leadership, since all living organizational systems require leadership.
>
> 2 - Leaders will encounter resistance as they pursue transformation
>
> "The deeper the change and the greater the amount of new learning required, the more resistance there will be and, thus, the greater the danger to those who lead."   Ronald Heifetz, <u>Leadership On The Line</u>
>
> 3 - We need the mind of Christ through the renewing of our minds, shifting our mindsets, attitudes, and perspectives so that we can recognize and then engage the transformation opportunities at hand.

Good Space involves head, heart, and hands.

However we describe ourselves in the entirety of who we are – we need to get our full selves into good space in order to move forward into the adaptive zone.

So, how do we know when we are there?

Well, here are clues that our church is not in the adaptive zone:
- Our conversation revolves around the past, nostalgically remembering when culture fed our churches new members
- Or, we are rushing as quickly as we can to snap back to exactly what our church was doing before the pandemic, believing this will restore balance and vitality
- Or, we are overwhelmed by the unprocessed and unresolved grief due to all the losses, making moving ahead feel like swimming through molasses

If we are there, we don't want to stay there, allowing these experiences to drag us down into inertia.

Instead, now is the time to do the work. Now is the time to do what it takes to recognize the adaptive opportunities staring us right in the face. Now is the time to renew our minds, coming alive to the possibilities embedded in the experience of following a risen Lord.

We want to be like our spiritual ancestors, those early Christ-followers who were scattered across the Middle East and Asia, exploding with the good news of the gospel as they went. We want to be like Christ-followers throughout history who have looked for God's presence and guidance in every life event. We yearn to be greater expressions of this body of Christ, God's Church…and now is our moment.

Let's do the work to get ourselves to good space, mindsets and attitudes that equip us for joining God's movement, God's unfolding mission flowing through our churches. Let's get ourselves, through the power of Christ, to good and adaptive space.

Clarifying The Why & What

The Why

Because God loves us
The incarnation of Jesus Christ demonstrates God's exceptional love for us and this world

Pivot Point

Before moving ahead, please write in your church's mission statement below. Thank you

The What

Transformation
- Transforming ordinary human beings into reflections of Jesus Christ.
- Transforming churches into greater expressions of the body of Christ.
- Transforming communities as Christ's reign comes on earth as it is in heaven
- Participating with God's transformation of individuals, churches, and this world is the primary calling of God's Church.

> "Jesus takes captive the imaginations of his followers and then replicates himself in them. In fact, we can sum up the task of discipleship as the life-long project of literally becoming like him, of becoming a little Jesus. But the whole process of becoming more like him moves quickly beyond the individual to the group and from there to a movement. Even a superficial reading of the New Testament indicates that it was Jesus' strategic intention to create a movement consisting of Christlike people inhabiting every possible nook and cranny of culture and society."
>
> Michael Frost & Alan Hirsch,
> *ReJesus: Remaking The Church In Our Founder's Image, 2022*

The Way of Transforming Faith
- God loves God's Church more than any of us
- The Church is a primary instrument of God's transformation of planet earth toward the reign/kingdom of God
- God has chosen to partner with humankind toward the reign/kingdom of God coming to earth
- God provides what we need to do what God calls us to do, including energy, time, and capacity

Discovery Point

What happened when you were asked to write in your church's mission statement above? Successful? Unsure? Couldn't find one? No problem?

Every church has a mission, spoken or unspoken, articulated or assumed. Whatever your church's mission statement, to what degree does your church pursue transformation as described in this Course? What might your answer mean for you and your church?

Gaining clarity on the Why and What positions churches to pursue the Way of Jesus. When churches are unsure or confused about their mission, the default trend is toward member-comfort. The following contrasting lists describe Member Comfort focused church culture versus Transformation focused church cultures.

MEMBER COMFORT	VS	TRANSFORMATION FOCUSED
Are people happy?		What's God doing in our community and how can we join God on mission?
Are we keeping people happy?		How well are we fulfilling God's call for us?
Is everyone comfortable?		Where are the examples of God's kingdom breaking out here?
Is anyone upset?		
Are there any problems to address to make people more comfortable?		What problems are holding us back from developing disciples or being missional?

 Discovery Point

While doing listening groups in a church who was engaged in visioning, I distinctly remember one person describing her perception of her church's mission...
"We just want to hold onto the members we have!"
(As opposed to doing anything that might discomfort them and cause them to leave)
Clearly, this person believed the mission of the church is Member Comfort (clearly not aligned with the Way of Jesus described in scripture). Again, where's your church on this? How proactive is your church's mission – rather than reactive, trying to please and keep membership?

Church Invitations

Every church is constantly extending invitations to those around it, consciously or not, intentionally or not. This is embedded in the nature of organizations.

Sometimes, our push back to the misguided over-emphasis on numerical growth in churches drives us to the opposite extreme, acting as if we do not want others to join us or like we have nothing to offer our communities. Perhaps a better way is to recenter ourselves in our primary purpose and calling, inviting others to partner with us in pursuing the beautiful Way of Jesus. The following are closer to compelling invitations.

- "Let's partner together to become more loving versions of ourselves." Brian D. McLaren
- "Let's partner together to raise our children in the Way of Jesus with strong community support."
- "We are partnering with our community in this 3 block area of our city, pursuing God's mission to transform our community. If you want to be a part of positive movement in our community, come partner with us."
- "We are being transformed as a result of participating with this church. Come journey with us and we will help each other become more Christlike while tilting this community toward the kingdom of God."

Uncompelling invitations (usually unspoken but communicated nonetheless)

- "We are desperate here, come help us save this church!"
- "O good, you have children and we need some younger people here."
- "We are so glad to see you. You look like an energetic person and we are ready to hand off leadership and responsibility to others."
- "Essentially, we are more interested in what you can do for us than what God or we can do for you."

This is why only compelling church will do.
Google dictionary definition of compelling: *"evoking interest, attention, or admiration in a powerfully irresistible way."*

This is the church at its best...life-giving, energizing, motivating, forward-moving. Compelling church is on a mission, pursuing something significant. Most of us are desperately hungry for this kind of church experience. We yearn to be caught up in the mission of God, transforming planet earth toward the kingdom of God.

Pivot Point

So what are we inviting ourselves and others into? For those who've been out for a while, what are we inviting them back to? Take this opportunity to identify the invitation(s) you want your church to give others in your community – invitations aligned with your understanding of mission.

Missional Movement First, Relationships Second
"They must challenge those who lack the courage to move forward due to a lack of faith or an inability to share in the vision...speak truth to power...at times, they must have the courage of conviction to choose the vision over relationships. Rarely will a congregation that embraces a new vision bring everyone along."
-Israel Galindo, *The Hidden Life Of Congregations*

Setting Expectations When Transformation Is The What
"As a result of participating with this church, I am becoming more Christlike in my attitudes, posture toward the world, thinking, relationships, and actions. Were I not part of this church, I suspect I would not be growing toward a more Christlike expression of myself."

Growing radically mission-focused
We do not have the luxury of mission-drift at this pivotal time in church life

Switching To Discovery Mode

We make the road by walking

We are on a journey
Going somewhere really good
Without a map, but with excellent navigational tools
Following one outstanding guide

> "A church which pitches its tents without constantly looking out for new horizons, which does not continually strike camp, is being untrue to its calling....(We must) play down our longing for certainty, accept what is risky, live by improvisation and experiment."
>
> Hans Kuhn, *On Being A Christian*, 1974

How Transformational Churches move into Discovery Mode

1 - Transformational churches move into discovery mode through cultivating the shared understanding that they are on a journey, moving forward into new lands

Pivot Point

We trust you are highly sensitized to the fact this is new territory for churches. We've never emerged from a pandemic, not experienced such high levels of volatility before during our lifetimes. Through this, we aim to remain true to the gospel, yet adapt to the changing landscape. How aware is your congregation of this reality? How willing are they to engage in adaptive transformation? How much do you have a shared understanding about what is – and how to respond?

Based on your answers, the next question is how to create shared understandings of what's happening. What might be your strategy for this? If you don't give this attention, disciples in your church will unconsciously undermine your efforts toward transformation, perceiving it as unnecessary.

This Course is designed to be a learning and growth experience for church leadership. At the same time, one can see how church leaders could use the Course content, Integration Guides, and videos for a learning and growth experience for the entire congregation. We are glad for you to design this yourself, adapting to your context. Others may want a Great ReEvaluation Coach to assist you, personalizing this for your congregation. This is an actionable next step for advancing the movement in your church.

Here are additional possibilities your leadership team might consider to stimulate your strategizing

- Use the videos to raise awareness
- Give verbal reports by lay leaders during worship about this Course
- Preach and teach about this subject
- Initiate a learning experience like this Course in your congregation
- Do a churchwide retreat on The Great ReEvaluation
- Invite denominational leaders to do presentations and facilitate discussions about the changing landscape
- Write articles for your newsletters and e-blasts on this subject

2 – Transformational churches in discovery mode translate institutional angst into motivational urgency

Angst ⟶ Gospel Filter ⟶ Motivational urgency

Institutional angst, concern over money, membership, and property, is real. And, if unaddressed can become the tail that wags the dog. With mission-drift, churches lapse into believing improving their metrics is their primary goal, the driving purpose of their church. As you know, fear-driven activity is rarely productive. O yes, it can jump start some churches, but it won't provide sustaining strength.

 Pivot Point

Consider doing this activity with your leadership team, setting aside an hour for uninterrupted engagement

- Collectively list (where you all can see) the fears and worries you carry concerning your church's situation
- Using the Bible and your foundational documents, identify the church's purpose as you collectively see it
- Next, using the Bible, identify the promises in scripture about God's empowerment of disciples and God's Church (may need to prepare some of these beforehand)
- Discuss the fact that institutional metrics are lag measures, lagging behind something else, indicators of something else. Discuss also the fact that we rarely can directly influence finances, membership, and participation.
- Based on your understanding of the church's purpose (making disciples, transforming ourselves and the world), consider what you can influence.
- Then consider collectively placing your energy there, translating angst into motivational energy based on our mission.

3 – Transformational churches in discovery mode give themselves permission and blessing to launch a season of discovery, experimenting and adapting

 Pivot Point

Some of you will remember when churches developed 15-year strategic plans. Then they shrunk to 10 years, then 5 years, and now long-term strategic planning is for 2-3 years. Why? Because our ministry contexts are changing so quickly. It's counter-productive to produce longer range plans which are outdated and irrelevant before we can implement.

Instead, becoming adaptive organizations who can adjust as we go, is far more productive. This takes adjustment in churches, since we have to use new muscles to function this way. One actionable process for moving forward is to

- Vision – pay attention to Holy Spirit clues or nudges or even obvious opportunities
- Do – Engage in the best way you can, Holy Experimenting
- Assess – Review how this went, how much progress toward mission advancement occurred, along with what was learned
- Refine – Improve and do more of this, shift directions and carry on, or totally set this aside and go another direction
- Repeat – Keep moving ahead

Here's the suggestion – Lead your church into a Season of Discovery wherein you designate a period of time, possibly one year, wherein you will pursue as many holy experiments as possible. Success is doing holy experiments, followed by the process described above. Imagine the movement in your church were you to do 5 holy experiments in one year, or 10, or 15!

When your leadership invites this approach, gaining collective agreement about a Season of Discovery, it sets the church free to be adaptive, often initiating increased energy and morale.

Role of Leadership When Switching To Discovery Mode
    -Reinforcing and rewarding every mission-congruent, transformational move
    -What is rewarded is reinforced, what is reinforced is valued
    -We are constantly training ourselves on what it means to be church

Pivot Point

Pause, taking note of the agendas in your lay leadership team meetings, staff meetings, and committee meetings. For many churches, much of the content of these meetings is focused on organizational metrics. How are our numbers? What are participation levels like? This focus literally shapes the values and priorities of the church body. Since these areas of church life receive the most attention, we are training ourselves to believe they are the most important.

Here's an opportunity to pivot. Consider prioritizing stories of transformation. Since your last meeting, what examples of people being transformed into greater reflections of Jesus have arisen? What examples of transformation in the larger community have come along? You get the idea. Sure, you may be awkward and unsure as you pursue this, yet what we recognize, lift up, and give our time and attention tends to grow.

Boldly Proceeding With Confidence

Biblical Promises

If we believed a small portion of the Biblical narrative, churches would be the most proactive, forward-moving, confident communities of people in the world. On nearly every page, Biblical authors are describing how God is faithful, equipping, and empowering far beyond our wildest imaginations.

 Discovery Point

Which Biblical promises have contributed to your faith journey? Which have served to sustain you during challenging times? Which empower you even now as you engage this Course? List any or as many as you can fit into the space below. We suggest your leadership team make time to hear from each person, making space for each to share one Biblical promise and why that one is meaningful to them.

Boldly – Definitions

    1 - without hesitation or fear in the face of risk or danger; courageously:

    To those who so boldly fought and died for our freedom, I apologize that so many have thrown it away.

    2 - without worrying about the opinion or judgment of others:

    He uttered his prayer loudly, boldly, not caring if the others overheard.

    3 - in a way that goes beyond usual limits of conventional thought or action; in a visionary or imaginative way:

    The new concert hall demonstrates that an intimate musical experience and boldly innovative architecture need not be in conflict.

                                                  Google Online Dictionary

Discovery Point

Discussing with your leadership team, look back over your church's history, identifying bold moves. Investigate several of these. What was the bold move? How did they happen? Why? What spiritual guidance or Biblical promise empowered those involved?

Now, reflect on your current church situation. Are bold moves underway even now? How ready are you as leaders to make bold moves? How willing would your church be to move boldly ahead? Consider what insights this brings you and then how this might shape your praying for your church.

Invigorated and energized by the challenges embedded in the current situation

When we move forward with confidence, knowing our why and what, we begin to resemble thriving churches. Recognizing thriving churches
- Know who they are and where they are going
- Disregard toxic criticism
- Avoid comparison thinking
- Remain mission-focused regardless of resistance
- Follow the energy

Remaining mission-focused

>Transformational leaders and their churches recognize resistance, push-back, and sabotage are inherent in change and growth processes. Rather than complain, they accept this as normal, expecting systems to prefer the status quo over change. Regardless, transformational leaders press on, knowing the value of growth exceeds the discomfort of growing pains.

 Discovery Point

"Transformational Leaders"
Spend some time reflection on this phrase or title. Spend some time with your leadership team reflecting together.

On a scale from 0-10, how much do you see yourselves as transformational leaders in your church? Explain your number to yourself and others.

What would it take for you to move up one number on this 0-10 scale? How ready are you to embrace this title, living into it more than before?

Imagine what could happen in and through your church when its leadership embodied bold transformational leadership.

Adapting As They Go

> The one competitive advantage of organizations in the year 2000 and beyond is the ability to learn the fastest.
>
> Peter Senge
> Describing the Learning Organization
> *The Fifth Discipline*

Proactive Sequencing Opening the Door to Ongoing Church Transformation

1 - Aligning structure with aspirational mission and vision

 Pivot Point

Now back to your mission statement. How fitting is your church's mission statement (or lack thereof) in light of this course? When our calling is transformation, how do mission statements reflect this? We could share many examples of helpful mission statements, but limiting this to one, here is the United Methodist worldwide communion mission statement:

Making Disciples For The Transformation of the World

Transformation is clearly the aspiration of this mission mantra.

So, this is an excellent time for you and your leadership to review your mission statement. When it clearly communicates your sense of calling and your aspiration, then affirm and use it! If it needs revision or a complete overhaul, launch that effort.

Insight – In the past, churches created multi-paragraph mission statements, believing they must include as much of their theology therein as possible. The outcome was irrelevance. Few churches used these wordy, burdensome statements for much of anything. Now, we recognize short, pithy, memorable mission mantras are far more helpful. So, don't spend years developing your mission mantra. Instead, it will likely come to you in a flash of insight. In fact, you might use the time between now and the next session in this Course to create the first drafts of your new mission mantra.

Mission Mantra Drafts:

You will need a clear and compelling mission in order to know what structure is needed.

2 - Short-term planning, annual with mid-year review or bi-annual

 Pivot Point

We've already described how long-range planning has diminished in usefulness. Instead, identifying your churches primary initiatives to pursue for this year, or even half-year, is more helpful. We recommend you use this opportunity to plan your planning. When will your leaders gather to identify initiatives? What process will you use? We recommend the process is brief, resulting in actionable initiatives. Build visioning and planning into your church's rhythm in order to give it priority.

3 - Streamlining and simplifying their structure, with an eye toward functionality

Pivot Point

Once your know where you are going (Mission Mantra, Initiatives To Pursue), then you are well-positioned to evaluate your structure: lay leadership team structure, committees, ministry teams, personnel. How well does the way your church does what it does align with your mission and initiatives? If you want to align your structure, consider the who, how, and when followed by initiating this work. Also, recognize that after this first alignment, your church will constantly be adjusting its structure as needed, improving as you go and learn and transform.

4 - Conducting Holy Experiments

Pivot Point

Please list your next 3 holy experiments below
1

2

3

Thriving Churches

Clergy and lay leaders form a leadership team, not only a management team

Value mission-congruent movement over organizational sameness
Thriving churches value mission-congruent movement over organizational sameness and member comfort. In fact, they recognize the counter-intuitive dynamic at play when disciple-developing missional progress dethrones the status quo from its idolatrous place of first priority.

Congregations that are growing (numerically) and spiritually vital are likely to:
- Have strong leadership that fits well with the participants
- Have a clear and compelling mission
- Be innovative and open to change
- Be active in the local community
- Have more vibrant worship that is thought-provoking and stimulating
- Have a community of participants that represents a diversity of ages, genders, races and other differences
- Be good at incorporating new people
- Have significant lay involvement, including contributing financially and volunteering

Researchers' observations
Congregational Life Survey
Hartford International University

Thriving Churches and their leadership are over it. They are engaging this present moment because they are moving beyond these six church energy-drainers

1. Believing or pretending the current context hasn't really changed
2. Allowing nostalgia to drive current efforts
3. Viewing young families as strategy, not mission
4. Gathering around something other than the Way of Jesus
5. Maintaining a reactive and defensive posture toward the current situation
6. Allowing traditionalism and worn-out activities to continue

Indicators Your Church is in the Adaptive Zone
Or, What Congregational Readiness Looks Like
- Most of the church moves forward with change rather than leaving, or threatening to do so
- Change initiatives are actually approved through the church governance system
- Most of the congregation is willing to trust leadership when uncomfortable change is recommended and pursued (BOD)
- The discomfort which comes from adaptive change is accepted as a normal part of church life
- There is an environment of holy restlessness
- Excessive talk about the good old days decreases while conversation about the present and future increases

Farming Church, Mark Tidsworth, 2017

Mark Tidsworth
Founder and Team Leader
Pinnacle Leadership Associates
www.pinnlead.com
markt@pinnlead.com
803-673-3634

Made in the USA
Middletown, DE
08 April 2023